Beginning to END

Sheep To Sweater

A Buddy Book

by

Julie Murray

ABDO
Publishing Company

VISIT US AT
www.abdopublishing.com

Published by ABDO Publishing Company, 4940 Viking Drive, Edina, Minnesota 55435.

Printed in the United States.

Coordinating Series Editor: Sarah Tieck
Contributing Editor: Michael P. Goecke
Graphic Design: Maria Hosley
Cover Photograph: Photos.com
Interior Photographs/Illustrations: Library of Congress, Media Bakery, Photos.com

Library of Congress Cataloging-in-Publication Data

Murray, Julie, 1969–
    Sheep to sweater / Julie Murray.
        p. cm. — (Beginning to end)
    Includes index.
    ISBN-13: 978-1-59679-914-1
    ISBN-10: 1-59679-914-5
    1. Sweaters—Juvenile literature. 2. Wool—Juvenile literature. 3. Yarn—Juvenile literature. 4. Sheep—Juvenile literature. I. Title.

TT825.M79 2006
687'.146—dc22

                                                                2006019900

Table Of Contents

Where Do Sweaters Come From?

Many people wear sweaters in cold weather. Look at the label of a sweater in your closet. You can see what kind of yarn it is made from.

Some sweaters are made from natural yarns, such as wool. Wool sweaters help keep the skin warm. They are soft to touch, too. Wool yarn is made from the **fleece** of sheep.

Wool yarn is used to make sweaters.
It is also used to make hats and scarves.

A Starting Point

There are more than 800 kinds of sheep. Some of these sheep live in the **wilderness**. But, many of them live on farms.

There are sheep farms all over the world. China and Australia have the most. On farms, sheep live outside. Their **fleece** keeps them warm and dry.

After sheep are sheared, they grow more fleece.

Fleece is also known as wool. Many farmers sell wool. Farmers shear, or cut off, the sheep's fleece. Sheep need to be sheared every year.

FUN Facts
Did you know...

♪ ♪ ♪ Mary had a little lamb....

... Some people have sheep as pets. Sheep are known as gentle animals.

My wool keeps me warm and dry.

... Wool is water-resistant. It can take in about 30 percent of its weight in water and not even feel damp!

Where's Old Ike?

President Wilson

… In 1918, sheep lived at the White House. They ate the grass on the White House lawn. President Woodrow Wilson sold their wool to help raise awareness about a wool shortage. The money was also used to help the Red Cross during World War I. One of President Wilson's sheep was named Old Ike. Old Ike was a ram, or a male sheep.

… Australia supplies most of the world's wool.

Australia is both a country and a continent.

The Makings Of Yarn

Wool that comes straight from sheep after shearing is called raw wool. Raw wool is the beginning of a sweater.

Trucks take the raw wool from farms. Then, they deliver it to a **factory**. At the factory, raw wool is manufactured into yarn. Manufacturing is a process where machines help make a product.

Farmers use a special tool to shear sheep.

One pound (.5 kg) of wool can be spun into 20 miles (32 km) of yarn. Yarn can be made into sweaters, scarves, socks, and other clothing.

Spinning A Yarn

There are many steps to prepare raw wool to be spun into yarn. First, **factory** workers wash the wool. They use big tubs of hot, soapy water. The workers also use **chemicals** to help clean it. This helps get the wool ready to become yarn.

When the washing is done, the wool is dried. There are different ways to do this. Some factories let the wool air dry. Others use machines to help with this process.

After a sheep is sheared, the raw wool is cleaned.

13

Next, carding happens. This process untangles wool and arranges it into a flat sheet. People used to do this by hand. But today, machines often do this job.

Next, tiny pieces of wool called fibers are spun into yarn. This yarn will be **woven** into **fabric** to make the sweater.

In 1912, people used machines like this one to card wool.

From Factory To Drawer

Machines at a **factory weave** the wool yarn into **fabric** to make sweaters or other things. People can also make fabric by hand or on a **loom**.

After the fabric has been made, the manufacturer does two processes. These are called fulling and finishing.

People knit wool yarn into sweaters.

To full the **fabric**, the manufacturer wets the fabric thoroughly and shrinks it. This helps improve the way the fabric feels. It also strengthens it.

To finish the fabric, the manufacturer brushes it. Sometimes, **chemicals** and color are added, too. Fulling and finishing help make wool fabric ready for people to wear. Then, the fabric can be made into clothing, such as sweaters.

Color is added to some wool as part of the finishing process.

After this, the sweaters are sold to stores. There, people buy them and take them home to wear.

Next time you put on a sweater, think about how it was made. Now you know that it all began with the wool of a sheep.

A sweater goes from the factory
to a store, where it is sold.

21

Can You Guess?

Q: Name the famous children's television show host who always put on a sweater at the start of each episode?

A: Mister Rogers

Q: What is one way people can make yarn into a sweater by hand?

A: Knitting

Important Words

chemical a substance that can cause reactions and changes.

fabric a cloth produced by weaving or knitting fibers together.

factory a business that uses machines to help with work.

fleece the wool coat of a sheep.

loom a tool used for weaving.

weave to make cloth by lacing yarn and fibers together on a loom.

wilderness wild, unsettled land.

Web Sites

To learn more, visit ABDO Publishing Company on the World Wide Web. Web site links about this topic are featured on our Book Links page. These links are routinely monitored and updated to provide the most current information available.

www.abdopublishing.com

Index